MEMBERS ONLY

MANICULE

hairless
unscarred
forever amputated
at the pressed cuff

darkness shades the palm
a small cave
hiding
a small eye

MEMBERS ONLY

MELINDA SMITH
CAREN FLORANCE

RECENT
WORK
PRESS

MANICULE POINT

FOREWORD

parliament: Middle English: from Old French *parlement* 'speaking'.

☞ This book has grown out of a collaboration between poet Melinda Smith and artist Caren Florance. The project began as a joint residency at Old Parliament House in Canberra, when the Museum of Australian Democracy and Craft ACT jointly invited artists to respond to the historic building's furnishings as the *Bespoke: Design for the People* exhibition, which ran from Nov 2014 for 12 months. Caren and Melinda selected a group of eight hand-lettered wooden signs as their inspiration, and ended up producing a series of eight corresponding text installations as well as some more traditional poems. The work, *Be Spoken To*, playfully rearranged the text of the original signs using a cut-up method, so that from originals like **Strictly Members Only** and **Take Care on Polished Floor** were born texts such as ***Members are not about to be polished for the visitors***. While playful in tone, the cut-ups engaged in a critical way with the text and context of the originals by exploring categories such as 'representatives', 'members' and 'visitors', and by drawing attention to the ultimately temporary nature of political and even physical structures. The finished works were themselves mounted on wooden signs and were placed across the room from the originals, as if 'in conversation' with them. The 'new' signs incorporated the colour scheme of the originals as well as using motifs from other parts of the 1927 'stripped classical' style building, designed by John Smith Murdoch.

Our collaborative project has also given birth to a print-performed letterpress artists' book, *1962: Be Spoken To*, which uses the year 1962 as a window into the life of the building and as a framework for eavesdropping on its voices. We selected 1962 because in that year indigenous Australians were granted the right to vote in Federal Elections regardless of their home state – in other words the parliament became, for the first time, (theoretically) capable of representing all Australians.

1962: Be Spoken To contains 12 main 'spreads', representing the 12 months of 1962, with each spread conceived as a room, using strong architectural motifs to frame and divide up the text. All of the sign text from the *Bespoke* exhibition is reproduced, but many additional poems were also created – most of them composed by rearranging existing text in some way, in keeping with the technique used for the exhibition. There are found poems and erasure poems from Hansard speeches and contemporary newspaper reports; each month has a theme, ranging from espionage to women's representation in parliament, and the original text was sourced from that month's records. The book also uses, as unifying elements and as commentary, rearranged text from the Wikipedia article on 'stripped classical architecture' and poems composed of anagrams of phrases like 'official secrets' and 'Cuban Missile Crisis'. As we listened to the voices heard in the building 55 years ago, we became aware of loud echoes in present-day debates ranging from public health to migrant accommodation. Some things have barely changed at all – and others have changed in very unpredictable ways. In composing and framing the texts, we have deliberately placed 1962 in conversation with the early 21st century. Eerily, these conversations are continuing: the 'official secrets' poem has quite suddenly come to seem like a poem about 'alternative facts', despite being written months before the phrase was ever uttered.

Which brings us to this book, *Members Only*. Herein are reproduced (and re-presented visually) all the poems from *1962: Be Spoken To*, but in a format much more easily held in the hand. Here too each month occupies its own section with its own theme. It is, in effect, the take-home version of the exhibition and the limited edition artists' book. In the interaction of the found poems with the surrounding anagrams, sign text, section titles, and manicules, there are a number of intricacies which will (we hope) repay multiple readings. Please enjoy.

FOREPOEMS

MUSEUM OF AUSTRALIAN DEMOCRACY

frozen bronze faces in the walls

typewriter carriages shuttling and chiming
cigar haze hanging in the cabinet room

red needle second-hands
     sweeping the clock faces
shadows of the union jack railings
     stretching their triangles over the carpet

mobs bristling with microphones
     rushing the front steps
the scratch of a fountain pen
     carving a slow signature

the tick of radiators
the glow of patient lamps

blowsy squelching of leather seats
     under the bottoms of schoolchildren
the smell of furniture wax

smoke from the tents outside

SECRET LIFE

In the taken country
in the house of half only
they made me a new body of wood
melted gold onto my face
set me in the thoroughfare
as a lesson, as a warning.
They made me no tongue to speak with.
Still I did my duty
by two generations:
my words flashed straight into their eyes.

Now my labour is over
I gather with my brothers and sisters.
We stand quietly, one-legged
in the room of stopped clocks
and exchange messages.

JANUARY

THE POINT OF THE PRESENT IS NOT TO BE THE PAST

IMPLICATE NOUN

THIS IS
STRIPPED CLASSICAL

J

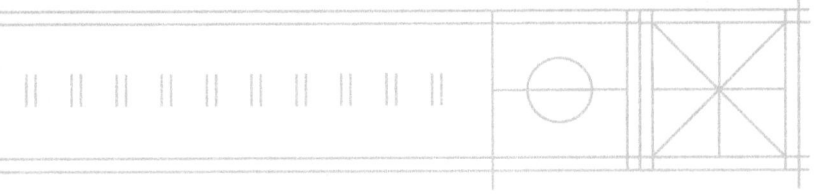

Scalped, I scar, split;
tepid carcass spills.
Rapids clip castles.
Ideals script claps,
placards list epics.
Piss scarlet. Placid
East calls. Pics drip,
drastic places slip.

Citadel's clasp rips.
Last relics dip caps,
art clasps disciple:
sacred plastic lips
spill sad practices.
It's all scrapped (sic).
(Clapped last crisis).
All scraped pics sit;

last cad prices lips.

FROM THIS HOUR HENCEFORTH AUSTRALIA

(The opening of Parliament House,

It is all a bit magical
(they do say
there are secret masonic symbols hidden
in the fabric of the building)
The Duke of York unlocks the doors with a *handsome golden key*,
unveils a bronze statue of his father with the merest
   brush of a finger
Dame Nellie Melba sweeps in, in her diamonds, sings
a verse of the Anthem (above the roar of the fly-past)
sits next to the Papal Ambassador.
The Ladies' Special Correspondent is agog at the Duchess'
   gorgeous toilette

The modern Wonder of wireless
conveyed a vivid impression of the ceremonies
to every part of the Commonwealth

There is a small religious service
to remind the twenty thousand assembled
Time, like an ever rolling stream / Bears all its sons away,
and thanks are given to *the God of our fathers,*
who has given us this fair land
as an inheritance

WILL BE GOVERNED FROM CANBERRA

Canberra, May 9th 1927)

Impressed with the building's *bold, yet austere white façade*
the reporter from the Hobart Mercury
calls the Kings-hall *utilitarian, missing the dignity of a dome,*
though the polished floor of Australian woods is allowed
    to be *beautiful*
(everyone loves the red leather in the Senate)

The Prime Minister speaks
May those who enter this door govern
with justice, reason and equal favour to all
in humility and without self-interest;
speak with the voice of those who sent them here – the voice
    of the People
A salute of guns booms outside.

Our man from Hobart, though,
sees through the razzle-dazzle
to the true future:
in Canberra there is apparently no speed limit,
and the continuous curves in the roads
make the movements of pedestrians
particularly hazardous.

USE THE POLISHED HOUR

POINT MANY

IN UPON

FEBRUARY

CARE FOR THE TIME BETWEEN

TO THE END

CLIMATE

FLOOD PLAIN

Polo if land?
Pool if land.

Foal plod in;
Lapin-flood.

Land of poli-...

Nod if a poll;
if poll 'no', ad.
I poll no fad.

I plan Flood
of old plain
(Plan of Idol,
plan of Lido)

and lo, I flop.

Fail! Pond lo!
A pond of ill.
Flap on Lido!
Lo, a flop! Din!!

Doll of pain.

Old, I no flap.
Fail? Plod on.
Flop. Ail. Nod.

Flood in lap.

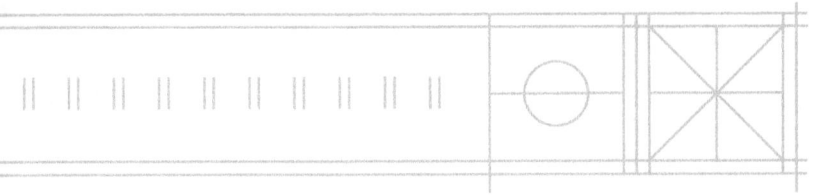

STAND ON THE TAKEN COUNTRY

View of the Molonglo, February 1962

This is progress, ugly and too slow, like life

Picture a little river
    banks well-wooded
        hay tall in the paddocks
            a little road curving through
                to dip and cross in a hollow, down there, squired
by spindly grey sticks of weathered telegraph poles.

The river has no future, or rather, its future is to be subsumed
    in the idea of a lake.
        Call it a dormant idea; sleeping these forty years.

        The embarrassment of Robert Menzies rouses it,
            unleashes the bulldozers at last.
    There is felling and gouging
moved earth heaped into putative islands named by committee.
A grand bridge rises to skim the treetops, two years ahead
    of its shore,
        soaring over nothing much, swirling with the dust of drought.
            Next month Menzies will unlock a chain
                and send a motorcade across.
                    A line of willows
                        clinging to a snake of sand
                              straggles to exit, stage right.

                Next year in spring, the valves will close
            on Scrivener Dam. Still no rain,
        the lake persisting as an abstraction,
      there will be billabongs, mosquitoes, acrimony;
months and months of Menzies intoning in his sleep
    trust, my people, trust
        the waters will come
           to cover this
                    wilderness we have made.

GALLERIES OF ONLY THE ONLY THE ONLY IN

MUNICIPAL

MARCH

THE SET APART ALLOWED PERMITTED THIS HOUSE

NOT THE NEXT

TONE

MAKE ME
A NEW BODY OF WOOD

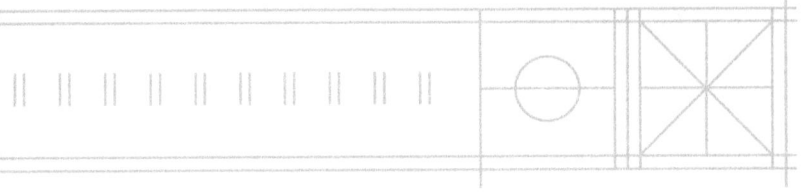

I, evil-onset,
I vilest one,
lie-oven. Sit…
I solve nite.

O, lie, invest,
vino elites!
See oil in TV!

Soviet line =
sieve: no lit,
no levities.

TV: I see lion!
Oil events? I
Lionise vet.
Eel visit on!

Voile inset
in Eve's toil.

One lives it
: vie on islet
: vote-in leis;
tie on veils.

O, elves in it!

Seen Tivoli.
Novelties? I
lose invite.

Loves tie-in.
Novelise it.

televisiOn

CONSTRUCTIVE

This is Grievance Day, and I have a grievance
about Bradfield Park.

The site was acquired by the Commonwealth in 1940
for a Royal Australian Air Force camp
the Commonwealth Government has taken over part
    as a migrant hostel

It is quite obvious
a service type of camp that is now 22 years old,
with the normal kind of huts that one finds in these places
of wood and galvanized iron, with thin walls and thin partitions,
and with, in effect, public latrines,
no matter how well painted the buildings might be, no matter
how the housewives might try to keep the huts clean, is simply
    not satisfactory
there are, of course, no individual yards in which young children
    can play.
Indeed, the children
run wild in the camp.

There is a school,–
a wood and iron structure with a leaky roof,
and all the rest of it.

I want to be constructive. I want to put forward an alternative.

I notice that the Minister for Immigration (Mr. Downer)
is in the House, and I hope that his reaction
will not be the stereotyped reaction of Ministers on matters
    of this kind.

There will be migrants coming in,
and they must be found some temporary accommodation
until they can go into permanent

a camp like that cannot go on forever. Indeed,
it should not go on for any longer at all.

the Commonwealth has got to consider
the building of decent accommodation
in the districts where migrants are likely ultimately
to live permanently
close to where their work is likely to be
their children could go to the schools
at which they would ultimately stay.
They could be integrated into the community
and could live in decent circumstances

There are many reasons, of course,
why we should encourage migrants to come here.
the Government has to do a great deal more
to make their lot easier.

something constructive
could be done.
the Minister for Immigration
should not continue to sponsor and perpetuate
what is really a slum, where decent people
should not be expected to live.

(*Henry Turner, 8 March*)

WOULD PLEASE LEAVES ON DURING

A NICOTINE

APRIL

MEMBERS NOTICE THE FLOOR THIS SESSION

LUMP

Carcinogenic

Nice cigar con.

Coercing, can I?

Nice crag icon,
nice car! Cog in
N. 'Iconic Grace':
nice ring. Coca?
(nice Coca grin)
Cocain? Cringe!
Gin, circa once.
Cognac nicer. I
cc coner; I gain
ice, caring con.

Ice narc, coin G
recon-ing ICAC.
Nice corgi can.
(I can, coercing).

I, cog in cancer

THE FACES OF THE DEAD

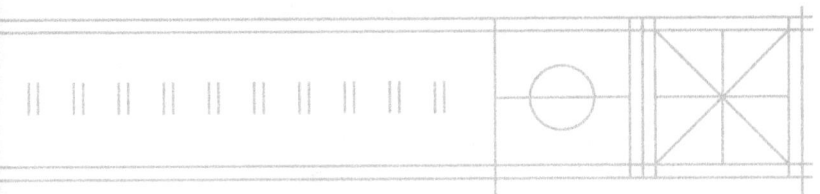

ARE EVERYWHERE

HEALTH, UPON NOTICE

Has the Minister's attention been drawn to
a report by the Royal College of Surgeons
after an investigation extending over three years,
that the death rate from lung cancer
rises steeply with the increasing consumption of cigarettes
and that heavy cigarette smokers
may have 30 times the death rate of non-smokers?

What action does the Minister propose
to warn the Australian community?

The Minister for Health has furnished the following replies:

The Royal College of Physicians is a most eminent body
its opinions have to be given very great weight.

The results of their study point to the need for a much greater
understanding by our young people
of the risks associated with smoking. It would be
   an excellent thing if
adequate instruction were provided in educational institutions,
especially high schools,
regarding the possible dangers to health resulting from smoking.

Properly explained information
would enable young people to be well
informed regarding the risks involved

before they commence smoking.

WOULD MEMBERS EXIT PARLIA

UNITE,

MAY

INDICATED

PLEASE

MENT

COMPLAIN

SET ME IN THE THOROUGHFARE

M

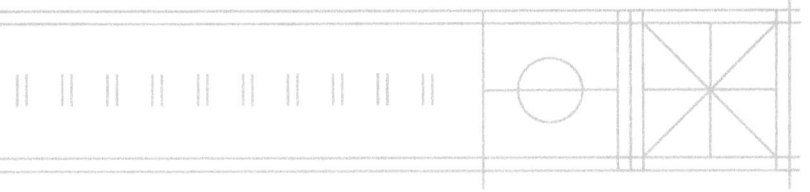

HOUSEWIVES

HI! SEE US VOW;
WIVE HOUSES
WHO SIEVE US:

EVE WHO IS US,
SHE WOVE US. I
USE, VIE, SHOW,
VIE, SEW… UH, SO…

EVES? WHO, US? I
VIEW HOUSES
VIEW SHOES, U
SHOE-WIVE US

HE VIEWS US. O.

VOW ISSUE, EH?

HE SUES, I VOW;
HE VOWS, I SUE.

A VALEDICTION

(from the valedictory speech of Sen. Agnes Robertson of the Country Party, on her retirement from politics after 12 years of service).

Now to my story.

It is about a girl who was to be married.
She said to her father,
"I shall be so nervous
I will faint as you walk me down the aisle".

Her father said: "That is a stupid way
to look at it. You will be quite all right
if you just fix your mind

on three things - the aisle,
the altar
which you are approaching
and the hymn
that the people in the church will be singing".

His daughter replied, "That is a great idea:

                                        I'll
                                        alter
                                        him".

She went down the aisle
quite bravely
with that thought in her mind.
I think we all come into the Parliament
thinking to ourselves,

"I'll alter
this and I'll alter
that". But things do not

always
work out
quite like that.

Some one suggested once
I ought to appear in films.

I think now that perhaps I shall
when you are watching television
you may see me
imitating
some of the things
that are done here.

ONLY ABOUT
PUBLIC
APPREC[IATION]
TAKE NO
MEMBERS
REPRESENTATIVES.
ARE STRICTLY

POLICEMAN

JUNE

HALF THE
ARE
ATED.
NOTICE.
ARE ONLY
REPRESENTATIVES
VISITORS

UNIT

I AM A LESSON,

J

I AM A WARNING

Partial men.
Male in. Part
man, part lie
(rampant lie).

Rant, lie, map,
lie, mar, pant.
Mantra pile.

Real man pit
in a trample
armpit lane
latrine map.

I arm planet
I mar planet
man at peril

: remap at nil.

PARLIAMENT

SKY FLASH CANBERRA 6.16 pm Wed 20 Jun 1962

a bright orange flash
filled the sky
north-east

No authorities were able to give
a satisfactory ex-planation
People said it lasted four or five seconds

Air traffic control officers at Canberra Airport reported
no air-craft in the vicinity
a glow rather than a flash

One woman said
it looked for a moment as if
the whole of Civic was on fire

the flash appeared from the direction of the coast
about the scheduled firing time of the U.S. high altitude tests
However, later reports said this test had failed

REMAINS A MYSTERY

JULY

REPRESENTATIVES ARE NOT ABOUT TO BE POLISHED FOR THE VISITORS

NO MALICE INPUT

I DID MY DUTY BY GENERATIONS

VOTES FOR ABORIGINES

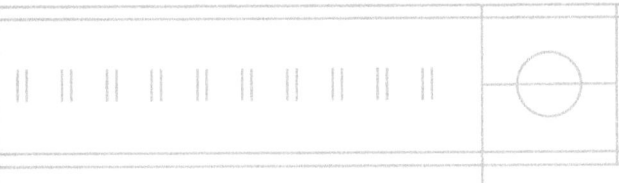

Forebears got vision.

Barefoot. Gives irons.

Givers of baronies to
fogies on riverboats.

Abortive griefs, soon
brave foes rising too.

Beaters forgo vision
or forgive obeisants.

Observatories in fog,
I forge observations.

Taboo grief versions,
of bias, too, reversing.

Fine brave riots go so…

Bereaving of roots is
roosting above fires.

marvellous

(*from the* Hobart Mercury, *10 May 1927, describing the opening of Parliament House, Canberra, the day before*)

the Royal party was not timed to arrive until
    nearly a quarter to eleven
practically the entire body of spectators had arrived
    by half past nine
nearly everyone
making wild guesses at the identity of
    uniformed and robed figures
as they mounted the steps.
(mainly humorous but good-natured)
an occasional acid undertone in some of the comment
(whole ceremony arranged for the comfort of a few, little regard
    for the remainder)
During the wait a great deal of interest was taken
in the appearance near the east stand
of an aborigine – a member of the Gundagai tribe,
a well-known character in the district, named Marvellous.
He was very old and grey, and ruggedly picturesque
determined to go his own way, in spite of the arguments
of two inspectors and one sergeant of police.
Immediately, and instinctively, the crowd on the stands rallied
    to his side
(choruses of advice and encouragement
    for him to do as he pleased).
A well-known clergyman stood and called out that the native
had a better right than any man present
to be on the steps of the House of Parliament
and in the Senate during the ceremony.
The old man's persistence, and the sympathy of the crowd,
won him an excellent position, and also
a shower of small change.

TAKING PHOTO OF SERJEANT-

MOLE UNIT

AUGUST

GRAPHS

AT ARMS

NOT

APPRECIATED

PANIC

EXCHANGE MESSAGES

Secret officials:

        Liars' Office ; sect.
        Ascetic ref foils
        scaliest officer.

        FOI scarcest file.

Sift fascicle ore;
foil access. Refit.
If accosts, refile.
Score if facts lie.
Sacrifice self to
cosier facelifts.

(So sacrifice left –
Coerce fails? Fist.)

        'Fiasco!', cries left

        Crate of files (sic) –
        fierce fact silos.

I see facts frolic;
scoff raciest lie:

    CAFÉ SITES FROLIC

                                      TORIES CLIFF CASE

    FIFI LACE ESCORTS

        CRISES AFFECT OIL

Crisis! Efface lot!
Clear its offices!

Elastic coffers. I
lease critics off.

OFFICIAL SECRETS

|| || || || || || || || || ||

Lie cries of facts,
so fact cries life.

(Life is core facts)

CORE FASCIST FILE

FOREST CALCIFIES

Fact: fire is close.
Face is set. Frolic.

Redfellows

(William Charles Wentworth, 30 August)

I **direct the attention** of the House **once again**
to the Communist school at Minto.

the Attorney-General has revealed **certain facts**
but he is not prepared at this stage to reveal certain **other** facts

it is essential to reveal **all** the facts

The Opposition says, "What rot!"
because their policy is to **cover up** for the Communists.

at Minto,
The so-called bush lovers' club
is actually a **Communist university**.

This kind of **subversion** is going on
and it is time
that the lid was taken off.

Does the Labour Party regard them as acceptable **bedfellows**?

These are not just **anonymous people**.
These are **individual traitors**
do you not think that they are Soviet agents still?

honorable gentlemen **opposite** are
operating as a kind of **rearguard** for the Communist Party,
by sneers, jeers and catcalls

the Communist Party
and its **machinations**
are getting altogether **too free** a hand.

SEPTEMBER

DOOR REQUESTED HERE BY VARIOUS MEMBERS

PNEUMATIC LION

Gough Whitlam.

I'm law-goth. Hug?
Ah, go with glum:
two-gal-hug him!

Might hug AWOL.

High-low gamut,
tough whim lag.

I glow. Math? Ugh!
Might laugh. Ow.

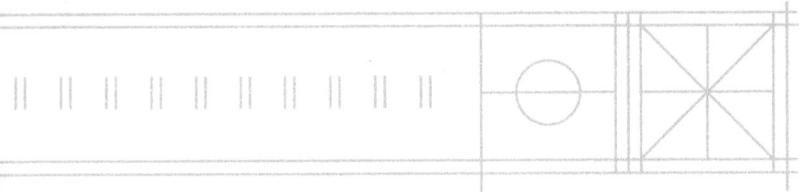

MY WORDS
FLASH STRAIGHT
INTO THEIR EYES

IT'S TIME

bearing the weight of the clock
everything tensed, ready for the bell,
the red light, the green light, the voice
issuing from the wooden box
– until that moment
in this room it is always
two minutes past two
and at the same time
it is always
one minute to eight

THE NEXT
IS LONGER T[

PUNCTILIO

OCTOBER

FLOOR DOWN
AN THE HOUSE

AMEN

TIME IS A RED NEEDLE SWEEPING A CIRCLE

O

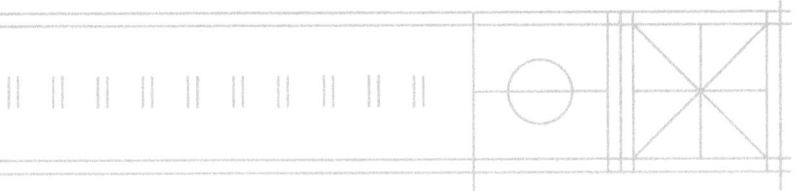

CUBAN MISSILE CRISIS

Basic miniscule sirs,
sissies incur a climb:
cubical rises in Isms.
Irascible scums, I sin!

Bless! Is a mini circus!
A clinic misuses ribs;
a cur sinicises limbs;
a sinus brims icicles.

Run miles! CIA is ICB-SS!
Cubicle is. . .. Siren!   Miss?

I, sinus, becalm crisis.
Ascribes nil; is music.
Incur a seismic bliss.

CLASSIC ERASE

Wars

became

monumental

all over

an ideal response to a

world

save

the expense

PHOTOGRAPHS
IN THE CHAMBER
ROOMS REMAIN
GALLERIES ABOUT

MUNITION

NOVEMBER

OF THE PAST

OF LEAVES

STRICTLY

GALLERIES

PLACE

Coma not memoir.
Mammon coo rite.
Moot memo cairn.
Moronic team om.

Aim to commoner,
am emotion corm,
am income motor.

Commit no more. A
Timor moon came.
Moon: macro time.

Moot. Memoir can
arm commie. Onto
it. More common: a
manic tome room.
Me, atomic moron,

coma. Monitor me.

COMMEMORATION

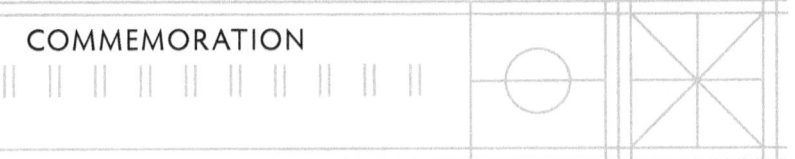

I HAVE NO TONGUE TO SPEAK WITH

what you get when you search for silence

one of his colleagues has gone into a significant silence
to silence us, but this is having no effect

listen in silence
spoken and heard in silence

the Prime Minister has observed an unusual silence on this matter.
an old Australian play, written many years ago, called

The honourable member talked about the silence of Dean Maitland.
of Arthur Calwell is the more remarkable aspect of this matter

I received a certain amount of ridicule, and a certain amount of
there is a period of awful silence while research is carried out, and
out of the silence into which he has preferred to enter

I am also conscious of the silence,
that there was silence. That is the answer about the £10,000.

There was
'The Silence of Dean Maitland'

The silence

scorn by silence
the soldier continues

DECEMBER

EXCLUSIVE PRIVATE SCHOOL EXIT HERE

PLUME INACTION

MY AIR IS
A FUG OF CIGAR

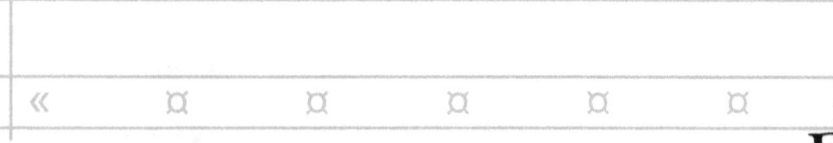

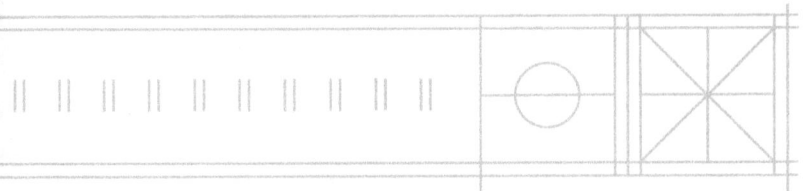

Robert Menzies

Robert Menzies,
sterner zombie
breezes into Mr,
rezones timbre

restore biz men
rezone Ms tribe

bronzes tire me

STARVED CLASSICAL

Between
the stripped standard
and the world.
Used.
Straddle and part.
Money works
by detail.

NOTES ON THE TEXT

"HR Hansard" = Commonwealth Parliament of Australia House of Representatives Hansard
"Senate Hansard" = Commonwealth Parliament of Australia Senate Hansard

FOREPOEMS: 'Manicule', 'Museum of Australian Democracy' and 'Secret Life' appeared in the Bespoke exhibition at the Museum of Australian Democracy, Old Parliament House, 2014–2015, as part of the collaborative work *Be Spoken To*.

JANUARY: 'From this hour henceforth Australia will be governed from Canberra': title and words in italics from *The Hobart Mercury*, 10th May, 1927

FEBRUARY: 'View of the Molonglo, February 1962' is indebted to the photographs of Richard Clough in his 'Collection of slides illustrating the design, construction and landscaping of Lake Burley Griffin', viewed via Trove www.nla.gov.au/trove

MARCH: 'Constructive' is a found poem from HR Hansard, Thurs 8 March 1962, Speaker: TURNER, Henry

APRIL: 'Health, upon notice' is a found poem from HR Hansard, Wed 4 April 1962, Questioner: WARD, Edward; Responder: SWARTZ, Reginald.

MAY: 'A Valediction' is a found poem from Senate Hansard, Thurs 17 May 1962, Speaker: ROBERTSON, Agnes. A Western Australian Senator, and the Liberal Party's first woman Senator, Sen. Robertson was dumped in 1955 and replaced with a younger male candidate, so she ran on the Country Party ticket instead and duly became the Country Party's first woman Senator (http://adb.anu.edu.au/biography/robertson-agnes-robertson-11540). At the time of her retirement in 1962 there were five female Senators (across all parties) and no female members of the House of Representatives. In fact there were no women in the Reps for a period of 15 years extending from 1951 to 1966.

JUNE: 'SKY FLASH Canberra 6.16 pm Wed 20 Jun 1962' is a found poem from *The Canberra Times*, Thurs 21 Jun 1962.

JULY: 'Marvellous' is a found poem which uses only the text of an article in the *Hobart Mercury*, 10 May 1927. The man named as Marvellous by the article is actually more likely to have been Jimmy Clements (sometimes called 'King Billy') rather than John Noble (sometimes known as 'Marvellous'). Both men were present at the opening ceremony, and sources disagree as to which of them was involved in the incident described in this poem.

AUGUST: 'Redfellows' is a found poem from HR Hansard, Thurs 30 August 1962, Speaker: WENTWORTH, William Charles

SEPTEMBER: 'It's Time', an original poem, appeared in the Bespoke exhibition at the Museum of Australian Democracy, Old Parliament House, 2014–2015, as part of the collaborative work *Be Spoken To*.

OCTOBER: 'Classic Erase' is an erasure poem from the text of the Wikipedia article on 'Stripped Classicism' https://en.wikipedia.org/wiki/Stripped_Classicism

NOVEMBER: 'What you get when you search for silence' is a found poem composed of the results of a search for the word 'silence' in HR Hansard in the month of November 1962.

DECEMBER: 'Starved classical' is an erasure poem from the text of the Wikipedia article on 'Stripped Classicism' https://en.wikipedia.org/wiki/Stripped_Classicism

CAREN FLORANCE is a Canberra-based artist who makes print- and book-related work, often under the imprint of Ampersand Duck. She has degrees in English Literature and Visual Arts. She teaches book arts and typography and is a freelance designer. This project is part of her doctoral studies at the University of Canberra. Her work is collected by national and international institutions, mostly libraries.

MELINDA SMITH won the Australian Prime Minister's Literary Award for her fourth book of poems, *Drag down to unlock or place an emergency call* (Pitt St Poetry, 2013). Her work has been widely anthologised both inside and outside Australia and has been translated into languages including Indonesian and Italian. She is based in the ACT and is currently poetry editor of *The Canberra Times*.

First published in 2017 by Recent Work Press and Ampersand Duck

This publication is copyright. Apart from any fair dealing for the purpose of private study, research, criticism or review, as permitted under the Copyright Act 1968, no part may be reproduced by any process without written permission. Enquiries should be made to the publisher.

© Melinda Smith (poems) and Caren Florance (design): 2014–17.
Typeset in Garamond Pro, Hypatia Sans Pro, BalboaPlus and Cooper Std.

National Library of Australia Cataloguing-in-Publication entry

Title: Members Only /
           Melinda Smith and Caren Florance
ISBN: 978-0-99535-384-8 (paperback)
Subjects: Poetry--Australian.
           Poetry--21st century.
           History--Australian

Other Authors/Contributors:
           Smith, Melinda, 1971– author,
           Florance, Caren, 1967– artist.

This publication was enabled by the generous support of the University of Canberra Faculty of Arts & Design and the Australian Government via an Australian Postgraduate Award (Caren), the Prime Minister's Literary Award (Melinda), and the Bundanon Trust (Melinda). We would both like to thank Craft ACT and the Museum of Australian Democracy, particularly the MoAD Heritage conservation team.

#fundtrove #1962bespokento @ampersandduck @melindalsmith

www.ingramcontent.com/pod-product-compliance
Lightning Source LLC
Chambersburg PA
CBHW030456010526
44118CB00011B/962